Malawi

KEEPER OF THE TREES

WRITTEN BY ALAN TRUSSELL-CULLEN
ILLUSTRATED BY FABRICIO VANDEN BROECK

CelebrationPress

An Imprint of ScottForesman

It was a hot, hot day, and Malawi the baby elephant was in a bad mood.

Malawi wanted everyone to know she was in a bad mood, so she stamped over to the water hole. She splashed and thrashed around in the water until it turned brown and muddy.

But it didn't make Malawi feel any better.

Malawi still wanted everyone to know she was in a bad mood, so she stamped over to the only patch of green grass on the plains. She rolled over and over in the grass until it was flattened and crushed.

But it didn't make Malawi feel any better.

Malawi still wanted everyone to know she was in a bad mood, so she stamped over to the only tree on the plains. She leaned against the tree. Then she pushed and pushed until the tree fell over.

But it didn't make Malawi feel any better.

The next day the sun rose high in the sky. It was very, very hot. Malawi soon became very thirsty. She made her way down to the water hole. But the water was brown and muddy. Malawi couldn't drink.

Malawi soon became very hungry. She made her way to the only patch of fresh, green grass on the plains. But it was crushed and flattened. Malawi couldn't eat.

Malawi soon felt very hot. She made her way to
the only tree on the plains to sit in its shade.
But the tree was no longer standing. Malawi
couldn't find any shade from the sun.

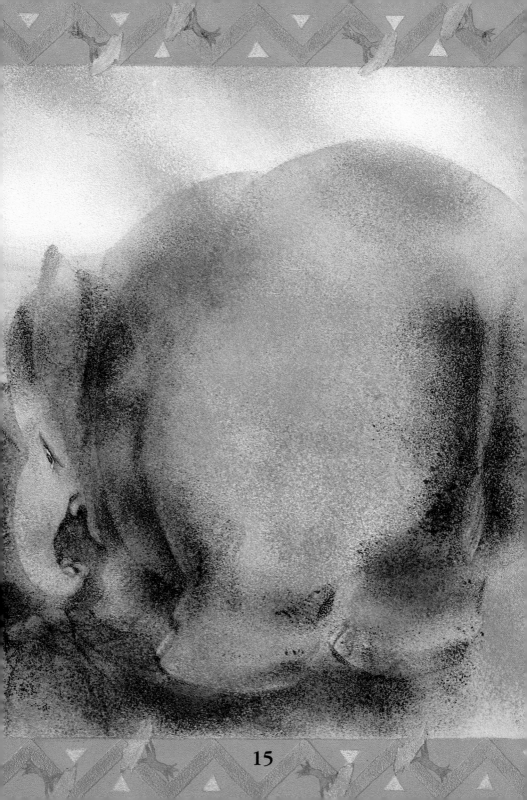

Just then an old hyena came along.

"Foolish Malawi," said the hyena. "When you have only one water hole, you must take care of it, because one day you will be thirsty. When you have only one patch of green grass, you must take care of it, because one day you will be hungry. And when you have only one tree, you must take care of it, because one day you will be in need of shade."

17

The old hyena looked closely at Malawi.
"Why must you do these things?" he asked.
"Because there is only one Earth."

Malawi lowered her head down. She was sorry
for what she had done.

From that day on, Malawi took care of the water hole so that the water was always clean and fresh for all the animals.

She took care of the soft, green grass so that all the animals would have food to eat.

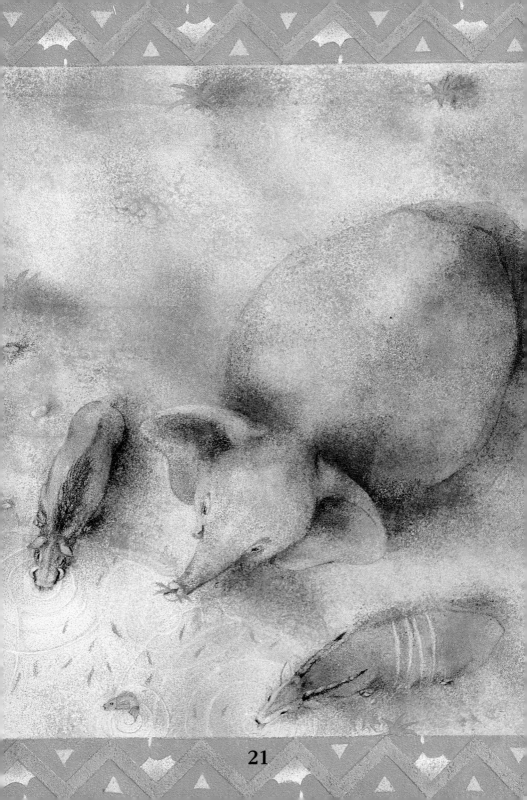

Malawi could not save the old tree, but she looked after the little seedlings that grew next to its trunk. She knew that in time all the birds would be able to sit on the branches and all the animals would be able to rest in the cool shade.

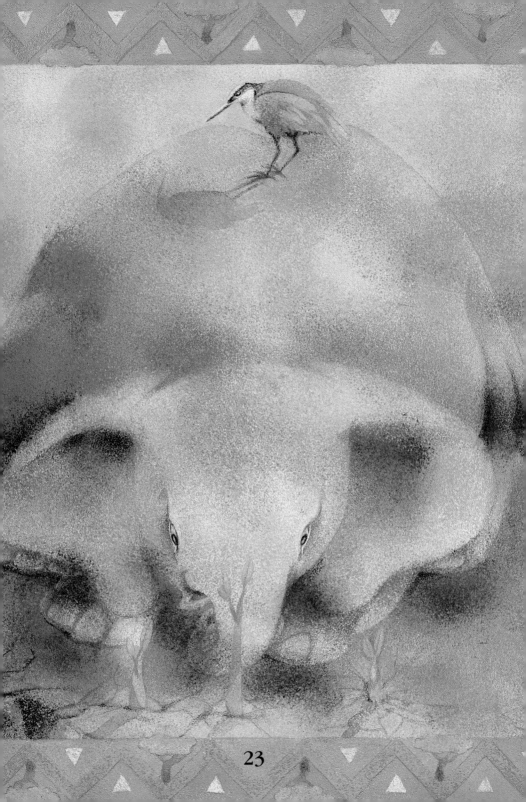

From then on, over and over, Malawi would tell all the animals: "There's only one Earth. Everyone must take care of it."